Why Boys and Girls Are Different

A Guide for the Christian Family

girls ages 3–5

CONCORDIA PUBLISHING HOUSE • SAINT LOUIS

Book 1 of the Learning about Sex Series
The titles in the series:

Acknowledgments

We wish to thank all medical, child development, and family life consultants who have assisted in the development, updating, and revising of the Learning about Sex series.

Copyright © 1982, 1988, 1995, 1998, 2008, 2015 Concordia Publishing House
3558 S. Jefferson Ave., St. Louis, MO 63118-3968
1-800-325-3040 • cph.org

From text originally written by Carol Greene

Illustrations by Michelle Dorenkamp

Scripture quotations from the ESV® Bible (The Holy Bible, English Standard Version®), copyright © 2001 by Crossway, a publishing ministry of Good News Publishers. Used by permission. All rights reserved.

Manufactured in Dongguan, China/055760/416281

5 6 7 8 9 10 11 12 13 14   31 30 29 28 27 26 25 24 23 22

Foreword

This book is one of a series of six that is designed to help parents communicate biblical values to their children in the area of sexuality and relationships. *Why Boys and Girls Are Different* is the first book in the series. It is written especially for girls ages three to five and, of course, for the parents, teachers, and other concerned grown-ups who will read the book to the child. (See "A Note to Grown-ups" at the end of the book for suggestions on using the book and ways to communicate Christian values in sex education in the home.)

Like its predecessor, this Learning about Sex series provides information about the mental, emotional, physical, and spiritual aspects of human sexuality. But more important, it does so from a distinctively Christian point of view in the context of our relationship to the God who created us and redeemed us in Jesus Christ. The series presents sex as another good gift from God and understands it within the context of our relationship to God and others.

Each book in the series is graded in vocabulary and in the amount of information it provides. It answers the questions that persons at each age level typically ask. Because children vary widely in their growth rates and interest levels, parents and other concerned adults will want to preview each book in the series, directing the child to the next graded book when she is ready for it.

In addition to reading each book, you can use them as starting points for casual conversation and when answering other questions a child might have.

This book can also be used as a mini-unit or as part of another course of study in a Christian preschool setting. Whenever the book is used in a class setting, it is important to let the parents know beforehand, since they have the primary responsibility for the sex education of their children. If used in a classroom setting, the books would be appropriate to read during a study of the story of creation or an "All about Me" and/or "Families" unit.

While parents will appreciate the help of the school and church, they will want to know what is being taught. As the Christian home and the Christian school and church work together, Christian values in sex education can be more effectively strengthened.

The Editors

I'm a girl.

God made me!

He's a boy.

God made him too!

God made you too. He did a good job, didn't He?

Each of us is *special*. We are all loved by God.

There is only one of you and only one of me in the whole world!

Each of us is *unique*. We are all precious to God. Isn't that amazing?

You are you. And I am me.

I like to hop.

I like the color yellow.

I like chocolate ice cream cones.

In some ways, we are the *same*. In some ways, we're not.

God made us that way. I like God's plans.

And I like you.

You are you. And he is he.

He likes to jump.

He likes the color red.

He likes vanilla ice cream cones.

In some ways, we are the same. In some ways, we're not.

God made us that way. I like God's plans.

And I like you. I like him too.

God made boys and girls with bodies that are the same in many ways.

God gave us eyes to see with

and ears to hear with

and noses to smell with

and mouths to talk and taste with.

God gave us hands and feet and fingers and toes.

He gave us laughter and minds to think with.

God made each one of us wonderful. He knew just what we needed.

God also made boys and girls *different* in some important ways.

God gave girls a vagina.

It is on the inside.

That is the best place for it.

God gave boys a penis and testicles.

They are on the outside.

That is the best place for them.

God gave boys and girls wonderful bodies. They are good the way they are.

All of God's gifts are good.

You know, God made a lot of girls,

and girls can do a lot of things.

His mother is a girl.

So are his grandma, sister, and cousin . . .

and that doctor

and that banker

and that painter

and the person driving that truck.

God blesses them with much that they can do.

God made a lot of boys too,

and boys can do a lot of things.

Her father is a boy.

So are her grandpa and her uncle . . .

and that firefighter

and that cook

and that teacher

and the person flying that plane.

God blesses them with much that they can do.

How did God make us
so that we can
do so many things?
I don't know. Let's ask.

God designed and created

you in a special way.

You see, sometimes a grown-up boy and a grown-up girl love each other very much. They want to be together and help each other for the rest of their lives. They decide to be a *family*. So, with God's blessing, they get married. Then, they decide they want a little baby to share their love.

Part of being a family is welcoming children into their lives. God planned that mommies and daddies are both needed for a new baby to be created. The baby grows inside its mother for nine months. It is safe and warm in her womb. Sometimes, when it wiggles and kicks, you can feel it from the outside.

God is blessing this growing family.

I think that's great!

Me too.

After nine months, the baby is born.

It comes out through the mother's vagina.

The whole family is very glad to see the new baby.

That is how God made YOU.

That is how He makes all people.

God blesses us in an important way.
He puts people in families.
That's so we can take care of one
another and always love one another,
no matter what.
Some families are small.

Some families are big.

There are many different kinds of families.

I thank God for my family.

Let's thank God for your family too!

God blesses us with families.

She likes to sing songs with her mother.

She likes to play ball with her brother.

She likes to listen to her grandma's stories.

She's glad God put her into a family.

Families do things together.

He likes to play with his sisters.

He likes to go fishing with his grandpa.

He likes to go bike riding with his dad.

What do YOU like to do with YOUR family?

God puts us into a church family too.
That's so we can take care of one another
and always love one another, no matter what.
People in church families share God's love.
They hear God's Word and sing His praises.

Some church families are small.

Some church families are big.

There are many different people in a church family.

But in some ways, we are the same.

We all are sinners. We all need Jesus to forgive us. And we forgive one another.

Families are a good place to make mistakes, because we know that

no matter what we do, we are loved.

I'm glad God put me into a church family.

I like to learn that Jesus is my Savior.

I like to sing songs about Jesus, who loves me.

I like to see my friends at church.

I like to pray to Jesus. He hears and helps me.

I like to know that God is always near.

What do YOU like about YOUR church family?

I'm a girl.

God made me!

He's a boy.

God made him too!

God loves each person specially.

He is our Father in heaven. We are His children.

God is so good to us. He knows what we need and takes care of us.

Thank God for all the blessings He gives to every girl and to every boy!

He loves us all. He loves YOU too!

One day, all who love and trust in Jesus will live with Him forever.

"I praise [God], for I am fearfully and wonderfully made. Wonderful are Your works!"

Psalm 139:14

The End

A Note to Grown-ups

We're all aware of the stereotypical adult responses to a toddler's first question about the differences between boys and girls. There may be embarrassment: "Er, uh, go ask your mother." There may be evasion: "Mommy thinks she hears the phone."

Of course, you aren't a stereotype. But you may be one of the many adults who prefer to approach their children's questions with the aid of other resources. This book is designed to provide that aid and to do so in a Christian context. We pray that this will be the beginning of ongoing open, honest, intentional communication with your child regarding God's magnificent design. But no one book can anticipate the needs of all preschoolers. Ultimately, adults must rely on their own sensitivity and common sense. A few pointers, however, may help.

First and foremost, remember that sexuality is far more than the reproductive organs with which each of us is born. Being male or female is a tremendous gift from God and colors almost everything we are and do. We are created by God for specific reasons! The sense of joy and wonder you feel in your own sexuality and that of your child is one of the most important things you can teach her.

Ideally, children would grow up in a home with two parents who openly show their love and respect for one another and for their children, where each person in the family is valued for who she or he is.

But this isn't an ideal world, and many single parents must cope without the aid of a spouse. If that is your situation, try to spend time with a special friend or relative of the other sex, and let your child be part of the interaction. Or try to spend time with a couple in your extended family or church. Models are important for young children.

Even if you are a bit nervous about talking about your child's sexuality, let her know that you're glad she came to you with questions. Curiosity is good; it helps us learn. Bear in mind that a child doesn't carry all the societal baggage attached to sex that adults do. Today, Sarah wants to know more about her vagina. Tomorrow, she may show equal curiosity about her teeth.

Listen carefully to the question, and be sure you understand it. (Remember the old joke? Hannah asks, "Mom, where did I come from?" Mom gives a carefully pre-planned lecture on reproduction. Hannah looks bored. It turns out her best friend came from Memphis, and Hannah just wants to know what city she came from.)

Once you understand the question, try to answer it in a precise, matter-of-fact way. If Sophia wants to know why Mrs. Blackwell's tummy is so fat, explain that

Mrs. Blackwell is going to have a baby. "But it isn't in her tummy. It's in a special place called the uterus, which God made for babies before they are born."

If Sophia follows this with another question, answer it with equal honesty, and continue to do so until her curiosity is satisfied. In general, it's best to answer no more than the child asks. But don't berate yourself later if you think you've said too much. Most small children will absorb only as much information as they can handle.

Don't be surprised, by the way, if Sophia repeats the same series of questions tomorrow or three weeks from now. For a number of psychological reasons, small children thrive on repetition. But do be sure that you're consistent in the answers you give. Also, be sure to use correct terminology with Sophia during such discussions. This will let her know that you're taking her quite seriously. It may also prevent embarrassment later.

An area of confusion for some children involves their genitals and their organs of elimination. "They're all in the same place," reasons Kiera. "And Mommy says to wash my hands after I go to the bathroom. So, they must all be dirty." If your child thinks like Kiera, explain that we wash our hands after going to the bathroom to get rid of any germs that are in a bowel movement. But that doesn't mean that any part of our body is dirty in a bad way. All the parts do just the job that God made them to do.

Unfortunately, you should also warn your child about the possibilities of abuse.

You might want to work this into a discussion of appropriate behavior. "Your body belongs to you, including those private parts that your swimming suit covers. You don't show those parts or touch them in public. And other people should not touch your private parts either. No one has a right to do that unless it's a nurse or a doctor helping you to be well or someone who cares for you by helping you to be clean. If anyone does touch your private parts, be sure to tell me. I want to keep you safe."

Our world is bombarded with sexual references and exploitation. Not even a preschooler can escape that completely. But your child's trust still remains in you. You are the real authority to her in almost every matter, including sexuality. Your joy and wonder, respect and love will awaken similar responses in your child. To counter cultural influences, be strong and consistent in communicating the miracle of God's design. The way God made us is just the way He knew it should be for our health and happiness.

Together, you and your child can marvel that "male and female He created them. . . . God saw everything that He had made, . . . and it was very good" (Genesis 1:27, 31). And you can rejoice that through Jesus' saving grace we can "see what kind of love the Father has given to us, that we should be called children of God" (1 John 3:1).